LINCOLN COUNTY SCHOOL DISTRICT NO. 2
ELEMENTARY MEDIA CENTERS
AFTON WY   83110

Children of the World

Spain

For their help in the preparation of *Children of the World, Spain* the editors
gratefully thank Blanca Kábana, Marquette University; the Embassy of
Spain (Canada), Ottawa; the Embassy of Spain (US), Washington, DC; the
International Institute of Wisconsin, Milwaukee; and the US Department of State,
Bureau of Public Affairs, Office of Public Communication, Washington, DC, for
unencumbered use of material in the public domain.

Library of Congress Cataloging-in-Publication Data

Yokoyama, Masami.
    Spain.

    (Children of the world)
    Summary: Presents the life of a girl and her family
in a village in southern Spain, describing her home
activities and the festivals, religious ceremonies,
and national holidays of her country.
    1. Spain—Social life and customs—Juvenile literature.
2. Children—Spain—Juvenile literature.   [1. Spain—
Social life and customs.   2. Family life—Spain]
I. Knowlton, MaryLee, 1946-   II. Sachner,
Mark, 1948-   III. Title.   IV. Series: Children
of the world (Milwaukee, Wis.)
DP48.Y65   1987   946   86-42808
ISBN 1-55532-188-7
ISBN 1-55532-163-1 (lib. bdg.)

North American edition first published in 1987 by

Gareth Stevens, Inc.
7317 West Green Tree Road   Milwaukee, Wisconsin 53223, USA

This work was originally published in shortened form consisting of section I only.
Photographs and original text copyright © 1986 by Masami Yokoyama.
First and originally published by Kaisei-sha Publishing Co., Ltd., Tokyo.
World English rights arranged with Kaisei-sha Publishing Co., Ltd. through
Japan Foreign-Rights Centre.

Typeset by Ries Graphics ltd., Milwaukee.
Design: Leanne Dillingham & Laurie Shock.
Map design: Gary Moseley.

4 5 6 7 8 9 92 91 90 89

Printed in the United States of America

Children of the World

Spain

Photography
by Masami
Yokoyama

Edited by
MaryLee Knowlton &
Mark J. Sachner

Gareth Stevens Publishing
Milwaukee

. . . a note about *Children of the World:*

The children of the world live in fishing towns and urban centers, on islands and in mountain valleys, on sheep ranches and fruit farms. This series follows one child in each country through the pattern of his or her life. Candid photographs show the children with their families, at school, at play, and in their communities. The text describes the dreams of the children and, often through their own words, tells how they see themselves and their lives.

Each book also explores events that are unique to the country in which the child lives, including festivals, religious ceremonies, and national holidays. The *Children of the World* series does more than tell about foreign countries. It introduces the children of each country and shows readers what it is like to be a child in that country.

. . . and about *Spain:*

Felisa lives in a village in Andalusia, a region of southern Spain. Her family farms in the agricultural area that is known for its grapes and olives. Everybody helps out, especially with housework. But people know how to enjoy themselves, too; Felisa and her friends dance in costume at religious and national celebrations.

To enhance this book's value in libraries and classrooms, comprehensive reference sections include up-to-date data about Spain's geography, demographics, language, currency, education, culture, industry, and natural resources. *Spain* also features a bibliography, research topics, activity projects, and discussions of such subjects as Madrid, the country's history, political system, ethnic and religious composition, and language.

The living conditions and experiences of children in Spain vary tremendously according to economic, environmental, and ethnic situations. The reference sections help bring to life for young readers the diversity and richness of the culture and heritage of Spain. Of particular interest are discussions of the variety of cultures that have made their presence felt in the language and tradition of Spain.

CONTENTS

"Hello, children of the world! We'd like to be your friends."

LIVING IN SPAIN:
Felisa, a Girl from the Wine Country

Felisa Díaz Martinez is a twelve-year-old girl from Spain. She lives in Almonte, a village in the Andalusian area in the south. The village of 10,000 people is made up of white-walled houses. They reflect the brilliant light of the sun.

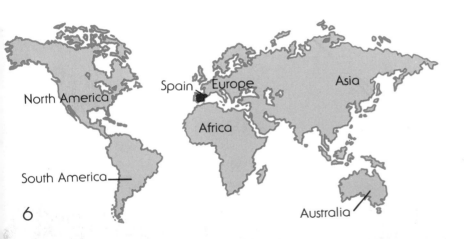

North America

Spain Europe

Asia

Africa

South America

Australia

6

Spain (Spanish State)

Atlantic Ocean

France

Madrid

Portugal

Med. Sea

Morocco

Algeria

Felisa's Family and Home

Felisa's family has eight people besides her — her father, Luis; her mother, Maria; her grandmother Rosa; and five brothers and sisters: Antonia, Pepi, José, Armando, and Vanessa.

A family photo taken in the living room: Pepi, José, Papá, Armando, Antonia, Felisa, Vanessa, and Mamá.

The patio off Felisa's house.

Rows of roofs of houses and the village church of Almonte. Many people come to the church *plaza* to relax and meet their friends.

Felisa's home is a typical Andalusian house. The outside walls are all painted white. Inside, the lower half of the walls is decorated with Spanish tiles. Throughout the house beautiful plants grow in large pots. The house is always cool and pleasant, because the shades are drawn to keep out the heat. Behind the house is the *patio*. All the villagers decorate their patios with plants and flowers in lovely pots.

The entrance to the patio in Felisa's house. The stained glass design is Arabian.

Farming for a Living

Felisa's father is a farmer. He grows a variety of fruits and vegetables. The family lives in the center of town, and the fields are outside of town. So Felisa's father is usually off to the fields before his children are up. He comes home for lunch after they are through eating. He eats alone and then joins the family to relax for an hour. Then it's back to school and work.

Spain is the third largest producer of wine, after France and Italy. Felisa's family grows wine grapes. In fall, when the grapes ripen, they are picked and dried in the sun. They are then squeezed in the *bodega*, the winery run by a local cooperative.

Relaxing in the dining room before returning to school and work: Armando, José, Vanessa, and Papá.

Felisa's father enjoys chilled beer or wine with his lunch.

A vineyard.

The village bodega, where wine is made.

Rows of wine barrels in the wine cellar.

The grape juice is kept in barrels to ferment. Some old wine has been kept in barrels for a hundred years. When the grape juice turns to wine, it is bottled, labelled, and shipped off to markets around the world.

13

The southern two-thirds of Spain, including Andalusia, is very hot and dry. Still, one-third of Spain's population works on the land. Also, much of Spain's economy is based on farming. Felisa's family grows other fruit besides grapes. They raise melons, pears, and peaches all year round. They grow this fruit in small quantities, but it's more than they need for the family. They sell what they don't eat to neighbors and friends. When customers come to buy fruit, Felisa's mother carries a scale into the living room. Soon the living room becomes a fruit market, and Mamá becomes the shopowner.

Neighbors come to buy fruit. The living room has become a fruit market!

Fresh fruit from the fields is kept on the patio.

Today a neighbor friend has come to buy melons and pears. Fresh fruit from the farm is kept on the patio. Felisa's mother asks her to bring in a melon. She chooses one that is perfectly ripe. The neighbors are happy buying their fruit from Felisa's mother. It is much tastier and cheaper than the fruit sold at the town market.

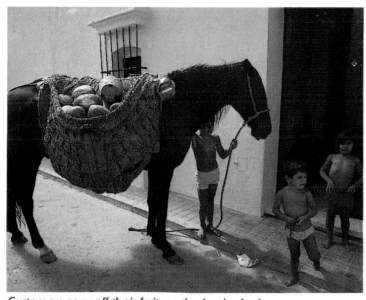
Customers carry off their fruit on the back of a horse.

The younger children come home for lunch.

Spanish Meals

Everybody comes home for lunch. This is the main meal of the day. When the food is ready, they take their plates to the kitchen, serve themselves, and return to the dining room to eat. Felisa's favorite food is *patatas fritas*, or fried potatoes, and *cocido*, a kind of meat and bean stew. She also loves *paella*, a rice dish with fish, shrimp, shellfish, or meat.

Mamá prepares a meal.

Felisa's breakfast is usually milk, coffee, and *galletas*, which are dry cookies. Sometimes she has fried pastry called *churro*, which she soaks in a chocolate drink. Around nine o'clock, the family has a very simple supper: soup, fruit, and sometimes an omelet and, for dessert, a piece of cheese. In Spain, an omelet is called a *tortilla*. This is different from a Mexican tortilla. In Mexico and Central America, a tortilla is a flat, thin cake made out of cornmeal, like a crepe.

José, Vanessa, Pepi, Felisa, and Armando enjoy their lunch.

The family relaxes together on the weekend. Pepi helps her mother curl her hair.

Color TV is quite expensive, and most homes in Spain have only black and white sets.

Shopping at the grocery. The shops have no signs on them. When the door is closed, you might not know that this is a store!

Helping Out at Home

It is Saturday, so the children are home from school. Felisa's mother asks her to do the family shopping. Her friend Monica drops by, and the two girls go to the market. The shops are crowded today because they will be closed on Sunday.

In Spain most stores close from 1:30 to 4:30 in the afternoon. The sun is at its peak during these hours, and its heat blazes onto the pavement. The village becomes very quiet. It's a good time to take a *siesta* (afternoon nap) or to rest and talk quietly with friends and family. Siestas are common in the summer months, when it is too hot to be active.

The girls buy snacks and detergent at the store.

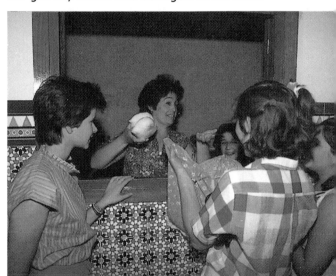

At the bakery.

On the way home. This is Felisa's street.

Felisa and Pepi clean up after a meal.

In a large family like Felisa's, all
the children have chores. Felisa
and Pepi wash dishes after each
meal. Felisa's special job is to
take care of the potted plants.
She is very proud of her roses
and carnations.

The children and their friend Irma care for the potted
plants out on the patio.

Felisa cleans the bathrooms.

The children's bathroom is off the patio.

Cleaning house is a big job. Felisa's house has so many rooms: kitchen, dining room, living room, sitting room, two bathrooms, and several bedrooms, plus a patio and upstairs veranda where laundry is dried. Today Felisa is in charge of cleaning the bathrooms. She sweeps and washes the floors. She makes sure the beautiful Spanish tiles gleam.

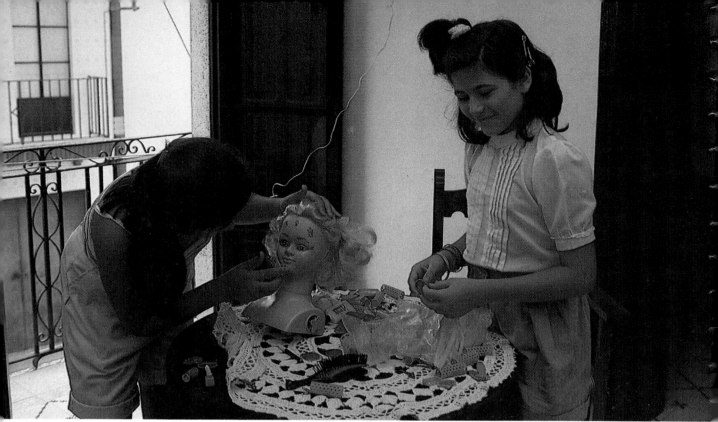

Pepi and Felisa play with their dolls.

Children's Play

Felisa loves to play with her dolls. Today she is doing up her blond doll. She curls her hair and puts on make-up. Even with eyeliner, blue eyeshadow, and pink lipstick, something is missing.

Pepi suggests adding pink and red pieces of shiny paper on the forehead and cheeks. The girls agree that the doll looks lovely.

Shiny paper — the perfect touch!

Making toys out of folded-up paper.

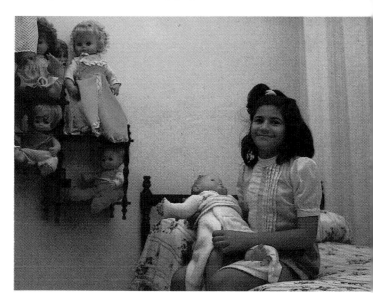

The girls' room.

Part of Pepi's and Felisa's doll collection.

Felisa's treasure boxes.

During the daytime, it's hot and the sun is very strong. That is why children from Andalusia usually do not play outdoors during the daytime. Instead, they watch TV, play games on the patio, or play with their dolls. When the sun begins to set, the voices of children are heard outside as they come out again to play. For children and grown-ups alike, this is the best time of the day, and everyone wants to be outdoors.

Felisa's favorite game is rubber-string jumping. It is called "saltar a la goma." Four girls form a square, one girl to each corner. Two hold a rubber string. The other two take turns jumping and landing with two feet on the string. It looks easy, but it is actually quite difficult to land with both feet on the thin string.

At Irma's house: Frozen ices taste delicious under the blazing sun.

Towards evening, the girls play saltar a la goma at Felisa's house.

José, Pepi, Felisa, Irma, and Vanessa clown for the camera on the rooftop of Felisa's home.

As time for the village festival approaches, the boys practice their horseback riding. Felisa watches them happily riding their horses, and she wishes she too could ride a horse.

The boys often play soccer and basketball. Soccer is very popular in Spain, and both grown-ups and children are great fans. When Felisa's father has a day off he goes to soccer matches. Though Spain has only two television stations, they broadcast lots of soccer games.

27

Playing games at Irma's house.

Besides soccer, Spanish TV shows a lot of *corridas de toros,* or bullfighting. The season runs from March through November. Bullfighting has a long history in Spain, dating back at least to 1080. It has many enthusiastic fans. Many Spaniards consider it their national sport. Little boys dream of becoming bullfighters. The famous Andalusian bullfighter, Pedro Romero, killed over 6000 bulls in 30 years.

The bulls killed in the bullring are sold at the next day's market with a label attached to them. The label reads, "la carne de los toros," the meat of the bulls. Felisa feels sorry for these bulls. She hates to watch them struggle against the bullfighter's attacks with spears and swords. She would like to see a kind of bullfight in which bulls do not have to be killed.

Pepi chooses a snack for merienda.

Between lunch and supper there is a snack time called *merienda*. This is the time of the day when Spaniards eat from the many sweets they make or buy. One favorite is jam or cheese spread on crusty Spanish bread called *bocadillo*. Another favorite is white bread served with a glass of milk and chocolate or some fruit. Felisa likes these sweets, as well as *pipas*, or sunflower seeds, for her merienda.

Felisa gets dressed for school. Vanessa is in no hurry to get up.

Mamá helps Armando wash up.

Morning at Felisa's House

Felisa's mother is busy every morning sending five children off to school. Nobody wants to get up till the last minute. Felisa shares a bedroom with her two older sisters. Every morning she wakes up to her mother's shout from downstairs. Then she begins her daily routine of deciding what to wear.

Felisa is very fussy about how she looks. She always wants to look good. She loves to wear her white boots with everything, so she puts them on first. Then she picks out her other clothes. When she's finished dressing, her mother ties a ribbon in her hair. She's ready for school.

◀ Antonia and Felisa are ready for school. Pepi is the last to get out of bed.

Felisa is dressed in style!

It's morning, and the children arrive at school.

Felisa's School

In Spain, children must attend school for eight years, from six to fourteen years old. Felisa's oldest sister, Antonia, is in high school. Vanessa, at four, is too young for school. The other four children — Pepi, 13, José, 10, Armando, 7, and Felisa — attend the Lope de Vega Primary School.

There are around one thousand students at Lope de Vega. The school year is from September through June. The students have a three-month summer vacation and breaks in December and around Easter. Otherwise, classes are held Monday through Friday. The school day begins at nine o'clock with a break for lunch at 12:30. Afternoon classes run from 3:00 to 5:00.

Felisa's 6th grade class.

Felisa is in the 6th grade. Her class has 31 students, both boys and girls. Their teacher, Doña Mercedes, is like a good friend. The students talk to her about their plans for the future as well as their studies. Felisa wants to be a news reporter. She dreams of the day when she will work for a newspaper and travel all over the world.

Chatting during the class break.

Lunch hour is long, from 12:30 to 3:00. The students who come from far away bring their lunch, but the others go back home to have lunch with their families. Felisa lives only a ten-minute walk from school. Like most of her schoolmates, she goes home for lunch.

During class breaks, the students chat or go out to play on the school grounds. Boys play soccer or basketball.

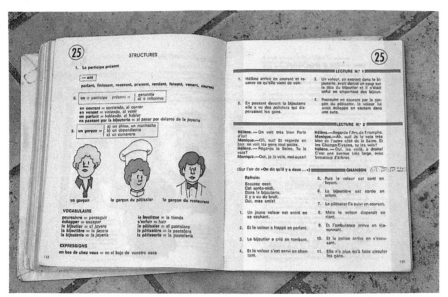

Felisa's French textbook.

Felisa is good at French. She loves her French classes and studies hard. But she does not like math. She wonders sometimes if there is any magic trick that would make her good at math. Her mother suggests studying. But that's not exactly what Felisa has in mind!

Science class.

Practicing flamenco dancing out on the school grounds.

When the time for the pilgrimage to Rocio draws near, every
seven years, many girls practice a lively flamenco dance
called *Sevillanas*. The Spanish have lovingly performed this
dance for a very long time. A group of students from the
school's student council brings a loudspeaker onto the school
grounds. The girls dance in casually formed groups. All the girls
are looking forward to dancing the Sevillanas in colorful folk
costumes at the Romeria del Rocio Festival. They must practice
hard to master the hand gestures, dance steps, and clicking of
castanets, or *castañuelas*.

Walking home with Antonia and Vanessa.

Today when Felisa comes out of school, she has a surprise. Her oldest sister, Antonia, and her littlest sister, Vanessa, are waiting for her. The older children are gone all day, and Vanessa sometimes gets lonesome at home. So when Antonia gets home early, she often brings Vanessa to meet the others. Pepi has a club meeting, and the boys would rather play with their friends. So the three sisters walk home together. The streets are decorated for the upcoming festival.

After school, Felisa hurries through her homework. She usually has about an hour of studying to do, and then she can play.

Felisa does homework in the living room.

Felisa keeps her school supplies in a living room cabinet.

37

The church is crowded for Mass.

A Spanish Festival

In the spring, there are many festivals throughout Spain. In the village of Almonte, the Romeria del Rocio is held annually on Pentecost. This is the seventh Sunday after Easter. This festival celebrates Mary, the mother of Jesus.

Pepi, Felisa, and Monica enjoy their churros from the church cafeteria.

This year in addition is the Rocio Chico, a festival that comes once in seven years. On this day, the villagers of Almonte take the statue of Mary, which has been in their church for nine months, back to the church in Rocio.

For weeks the village has bristled with excitement. The women have made paper flowers to deck the road the statue will follow. Gun salutes have been fired each morning and special masses said in the evening. Now the festival is here.

A long candle procession is led by the children.

Everyone gathers to escort the statue of Mary to Rocio.

The procession crosses fields of flowers, including amapola flowers.

Around three in the morning, the statue of Mary leaves the church in Almonte. It is carried by the men of the village. For the next seven years it will remain in Rocio, a village 10 miles (16 km) from Almonte.

The statue is wrapped in white cloth to keep it free of sand and dust. As it proceeds towards Rocio, the villagers sing songs. They will spend all night and all the next day bringing the statue back. Some join the procession in carts or on the backs of their donkeys.

The family heads for Rocio in a wagon with a roof of eucalyptus leaves.

Felisa's family joins the procession in a wagon pulled by their father's tractor. They carry baskets of food, sandwiches, egg tortillas, wine, beer, and cold drinks. They give food and drink to those tired from the long walk.

On the way they see Felisa's friend Eva. She is holding a bunch of crimson-red *amapola*, or poppy, flowers. She has picked them as offerings to Mary.

One week later is the Rocio Chico Festival. Rocio is a small village of only several hundred people. Today, though, it is packed with thousands of people who have come for the festival. For these three days, all cars are banned. The pilgrims travel by horse or oxcart to express their gratitude to Mary and to seek her blessing. Back in Almonte, it is like a ghost town.

Today, for a change, Felisa gets up early. Her mother helps her dress in a flamenco dress and fixes her hair with flowers and combs. Bright earrings dangle from her ears and she even wears a little make-up. Felisa feels like a princess!

Mass. Colorfully dressed people from all over Andalusia make the pilgrimage to Rocio.

People come in every kind of horse cart.

These people fill their cart with songs and laughter.

Some pilgrim groups number over three thousand!

People sing and dance in colorful costumes.

Everybody — grown-up and child alike — wears a colorful costume. They shoot off firecrackers, called *petardos,* and sing and dance in the streets. The music of tambourines, guitars, flutes, and drums resounds all day long. Parades of horses and carts pass slowly through the streets.

At last, the statue of Mary is brought out of the church and shown to the crowds. This is the high point of the festival. People run forward crying, "Viva Maria! Viva Maria!"

Perfect picnic weather!

An Afternoon Picnic

The weather is beautiful—just right for a picnic after school. Felisa, Pepi, Armando, and José head for their father's fields. Their mother has packed a special merienda. She has given them fresh ham sandwiches on the crusty bread, *pocadillo*. Felisa sticks them in a basket with a sweet melon, and they're off!

The children head for a clump of eucalyptus trees — the perfect spot for their merienda.

Papá's melon tastes delicious outdoors.

Pepi and Felisa enjoy each other's company in an avenue of trees.

The children walk through the village's row of white houses. They cross a stream and walk through a row of eucalyptus trees. Beyond them stretch field after field of farm crops.

It is late afternoon, but the sun is still high in the sky, shining brightly. Their stomachs tell them it is time to eat. They eat their food in the shade of the trees of their father's fields.

45

Heading home, the children meet a neighbor.

He has loaded his horse with melons from the fields, and now he, too, is heading home.

FOR YOUR INFORMATION: Spain

Official name: Estado España (es-TAH-doh es-PAHN-nia)
Spanish State

Capital: Madrid

History

The Ancient Iberian Invaders

Once a grouping of separate cities and kingdoms on the Iberian Peninsula, Spain's prehistoric civilizations date back to the Stone Age. Its recorded history starts around 1000 BC. The earliest known tribes entered the Iberian Peninsula from the north. Ancient peoples from Greece and the Middle East also invaded the peninsula.

The Romans in Hispania

By 39 BC, the Romans had conquered all of what they called *Hispania,* or Spain. The present Spanish language, religion, and laws all had their start in Roman Spain. In the 5th century AD, Spain was invaded by the Visigoths, who made Christianity the dominant religion in Spain. To this day, Spain is over 90% Roman Catholic.

Moorish Spain

In 711, Arabs sailed across the Strait of Gibraltar from North Africa into the Andalusian region of Spain. The Arabs were known as Moors. They conquered the Visigoths and stayed in Spain for another 700 years. Arabic language and culture had an impact on Spain that has remained through today. The Moors brought strong government and scientific advances to Spain. They also brought Islam. In general, Moorish culture and arts made Spain as much a Near Eastern nation as a European one. By 1492, the year Columbus sailed to the Americas, the Christians had taken back all but Granada from the Moors. And by 1512, all of Spain was once again Christian.

The Spanish Inquisition

Ferdinand and Isabella were the Catholic monarchs who in 1492 both defeated the Moors and launched Columbus' trip to the New World. They had also launched the Spanish Inquisition, in 1478. By 1492, both Muslims and Jews were being converted or expelled from Catholic Spain. This went on even as Columbus left for America. In time, the Inquisition turned more and more against other Catholics. And when Protestantism came into being in the 1500s, the Spanish Inquisition turned on Protestants. It was not until the early 1800s that the Inquisition died out completely.

The Rise and Decline of the Spanish Empire

From the early 16th century on, Spain became the largest empire in the world. In the New World, Spain conquered Mexico and Peru. In Europe and the Mediterranean,

Spain fought wars against France, Turkey, Holland, and Germany. By 1580, Spain had conquered all of Portugal and made it part of Spain. These wars made Spain the mightiest European power, but they were also long and costly. In 1588, Britain defeated Spain's once-mighty navy, the Spanish Armada. The decline of Spain's power had begun.

Spain lost even more power in the 17th and 18th centuries. Portugal became independent in 1640. Jamaica became British in 1655. France occupied much of Spain under Napoleon from 1808 to 1814. In the 19th century, Spain lost most of its American colonies. Spain lost Cuba, Puerto Rico, and the Philippines to the US in 1898 in the Spanish-American War.

The Twentieth Century and the Spanish Civil War

Spain stayed neutral during World War I amidst its own political troubles. From 1923 to 1930, General Primo de Rivera took power and set up a repressive military dictatorship. In 1931 a new Republic was established. In 1936, a nationally elected government took office. This election did not end the tensions inside Spain, however. In July, 1936, General Francisco Franco led a military uprising against the elected government. This uprising led to the Spanish Civil War, which cost over 600,000 lives.

Both sides in the Civil War received support from other nations, and many feel that this war set the stage for World War II. Franco's rebels were known as Nationalists. They received support from Fascist Italy and Nazi Germany. The government of Spain received support from the Soviet Union. The major Western democracies (France, Britain, the US) remained neutral.

Forces loyal to the Madrid government, or Republicans, included the International Brigades - 40,000 anti-Fascist volunteer fighters from Europe and North and South America. Spanish workers and peasants also defended the Madrid government. But in March, 1939, Franco took control of the government. He ruled for 36 years, until his death in 1975. By World War II, the USSR, France, Britain, and the US would be Allies fighting German and Italian fascism. Spain under Franco was officially neutral during World War II. But Franco's dictatorship was, like those of Italy and Nazi Germany, a Fascist one. Franco lent moral support to Germany and Italy.

Franco brought many Spaniards a sense of national pride and identity. But Spain paid a high price for its pride. Franco's dictatorship was repressive. It controlled the flow of information as well as the activities of workers and many others. It robbed Spaniards of many of their freedoms, both as individuals and as members of groups. It also cut Spain off politically, economically, and socially from Europe.

After Franco: a New Spain

Following World War II, Spain was not allowed into the United Nations until 1955, after Franco let the US build military bases on Spanish soil. Also, Spain did not become a member of the European Economic Community (EEC) until well after Franco's death.

When Franco died in 1975, Juan Carlos became king and chief of state. As king, Juan Carlos has done much to bring Spain back into the European community. Political reforms have made Spain a parliamentary democracy. Political parties and labor unions are once again legal. Socially and politically, Spain has rejoined the European community. But more challenges remain. Not only must Spain *live* with other European nations. It must also catch up economically and technologically with the rest of Western Europe.

Government

When Francisco Franco died in 1975, the new king, Juan Carlos, acted quickly but carefully to bring democracy back to Spain. By 1977, Juan Carlos had created a more open government and society, with changes such as these: the right to vote for all citizens over 18, freedom of assembly, the freeing of all nonviolent political prisoners, the legalization of labor unions and all political parties, including the Communists, and the first elections to the *Cortes* (parliament) since 1936. By 1978, Juan Carlos had given up his control of the government and the voters of Spain had approved a democratic constitution. This constitution made Spain a parliamentary monarchy, with an elected prime minister.

The 1978 constitution also divided Spain into 17 regions. Historically, each native region has long had its own identity. Now each region has its own flag and government. Some also have an official language in addition to Castilian, the official language in all of Spain. Each government is like a state or provincial government in the US and Canada. Each government is in charge of certain laws and services in its region. All 17 regions are under the central government in Madrid. There is conflict and debate among Spain's many elements. Some regions, such as the Basque region, have argued - and often fought - for independence. Each government plays a key role in its region's relations with the central government.

Today Spain is a social democracy, and the Franco era has left a bad feeling among many Spaniards. Many resent the help the US gave Franco so soon after World War II and feel that Spain should depend less on the US. Spain's government has close ties with the US and other Western governments. But it also values its independence. In 1986 Spaniards voted to keep Spain in NATO (the North Atlantic Treaty Organization). But they also voted to restrict Spain's military role in NATO, keep nuclear arms off Spanish soil, and reduce the US military in Spain.

Language

Among foreign languages, English is the most widely spoken in Spain today. But away from the big cities and tourist areas, even English is not very common. Castilian is the dialect of Spanish that began in the Castilian regions of Spain. It is also the official language of Spain. In addition to Castilian, there are other dialects and languages spoken in their native regions. About 17% of the people in Spain speak Catalan. In Spain under Franco, Catalan was banned. Today, it is taught in the schools. In addition to Catalan, about 7% speak Galician, and 2% speak Basque. These three languages are official languages for their regions.

A resident of a small village in La Mancha. The windmills have identified La Mancha for centuries. Many people outside of Spain know of them from Cervantes' *Don Quixote*, which was written in 1605.

The Basque language is unrelated to any other except, possibly, some in the Caucasus Mountains in Russia. Some people think it is the hardest language in the world. The sentence that says, "I give the boy the book," would be, in Basque, "Liburua mutilari ematen diot." The actual translation of these words is "Book the boy to in the act of giving I have it to him."

When Sephardic Jews were expelled from Spain in 1492, most settled in other countries around the Mediterranean. In time they added Hebrew to the Spanish they had taken with them. Later, they also added Turkish, Arabic, Greek, and Italian, depending on what countries they were in. They called this dialect *Ladino*. It is written in Hebrew letters, and many of its expressions are from the Spain of centuries ago. It is still used by some Sephardic Jews in Mediterranean communities.

Religion

Spain has been Catholic for centuries. It had once been Christian under the Romans and Visigoths. Then, under the Moors from the 8th to the 15th centuries, it was Muslim. Under Islam, Spain was more accepting of Jews than under Christianity.

Jews were persecuted by most European nations. But *Sephardic*, or Spanish Jewish, culture mostly flourished under Islam. In the 15th century, Spain became Catholic, and Jews and Muslims either became Christian or were expelled under the Spanish Inquisition. After the Jews and Muslims left Spain, many of their synagogues and mosques were used as churches. Today, some churches in Spain are still Arab in their design or have Hebrew letters carved in their walls.

During the Inquisition, people were persecuted for what the Church felt were failures of faith. The Inquisition spread throughout Europe in the 15th century, but it lasted into the 19th century in Spain. People of any faith but Catholicism were imprisoned, killed, or driven from the country. And in time, even Catholics suffered under the Inquisition. Today 99% of Spaniards are members of the Catholic Church. Since Franco's death, however, Spaniards have been free to join other churches.

Spanish life is deeply influenced by Catholic traditions. Each city and region has its own *fiesta*, often in honor of a patron saint. National holidays include at least seven religious holidays. Christmas is more religious and less commercial than in the US and Canada. Gifts are opened on January 6, the day of the arrival of the Wise Men.

Education

In Spain, all children from 6-14 must go to school. Following 8th grade, many quit school and look for work. But many also go on to school to prepare for a career or for college. Many boys over 14 and girls over 16 work and go to night school.

About 70% of the student population in Spain attends public schools. The rest go to private schools. Most private schools are run by the Catholic Church. Parents in middle and upper class families spend lots of money on education. In recent years, however, more and more parents are sending their children to public schools. The emphasis on primary education has produced a high literacy rate of 97%. Since the death of Franco, the education budget has doubled. The government is improving the quality of Spain's universities, which had been declining for many years.

Art and Culture

From the 8th through the 15th centuries, Spain was mainly Arab - and Muslim - under the Moors from North Africa. During this time, Arab art, literature, music, and architecture flourished in Spain. Even today, the influence of the Moors has made Spain unique among European countries. The arts showing an Arab influence are referred to as *Mudéjar*. This word comes from an Arabic word for Muslims who have been conquered by others.

During the Moorish era, Jewish religion and culture also flowered in Spain. Moorish Spain was home to many Sephardic, or Spanish Jewish, artists and writers. The mix of Hebrew and Arabic languages and cultures produced the Golden Age of Spain in Jewish literature. This age ended for Jews and Muslims alike when both groups were driven out of Spain by the Inquisition in 1492.

Spain is a country of great writers. In 1605, Cervantes wrote the world's first novel, *Don Quixote* (pronounced *kee-HOH-tay*). This story has been made into a play beloved by English-speaking people, "The Man of La Mancha." It tells of a man whose dreams are so strong, that he is able to convince others to believe in them, too. In more recent years, four Spanish writers have won the Nobel Prize.

Spanish music has a rich history. Lovers of fine music know the names of two of this century's greatest musicians, cellist Pablo Casals and guitarist Andres Segovia. De Falla composed "The Three Cornered Hat," an opera known by children in many countries. Some musicians were known for both composing and performing. Sarasate was a famous violinist who wrote beautiful Spanish dances and serenades.

The world of art has been greatly enriched by the work of Spanish painters. El Greco, Velázquez, and Goya are three painters from past centuries. The Prado, Spain's national art museum, has whole floors devoted to each of these artists. The painters of the 20th century are major figures in modern art. Picasso, Miro, Gris, and Dali are names you will see in museums in most major cities.

The Spanish are very proud of the influence their culture has had on the rest of the world. In Madrid, the Museo de América shows how the cultures of North, Central, and South America adopted Spanish ways. The museum has maps, paintings, tiles, tapestries, and religious objects.

Public support for the arts has increased since the death of Franco. European art collectors are buying new Spanish painting and sculpture. Spanish films win Academy Awards. The museums have been made free for Spanish citizens. The Prado is being remodeled after years of neglect. For many years, Spanish art was available only to the wealthy. But this has changed, and the people of Spain have eagerly embraced the culture many had only heard about.

Sports and Recreation

Spaniards are true *aficionados*, or fans, of sports. As in many countries, the favorite spectator sport is *fútbol*, or soccer. Stadiums in Barcelona and Madrid hold 100,000 and 135,000. In other cities, tens of thousands turn out to watch matches between different city teams. Since World War II, basketball has become popular, too. And in the last few years, baseball *(beisbol)* has become popular.

Most large Spanish cities also have *frontóns* where *jai-alai*, or *pelota*, is played. From the Basque region, jai-alai spread to the rest of Spain and to the Americas. The players strap curved baskets to their wrists. They use these baskets to throw a hard ball against a tall wall and then catch it. The ball speeds up each time it is thrown. The idea is to get your opponent to miss a catch. It has been called the fastest game in the world. It is exciting to watch, and in both Spain and America, fans usually bet money on players and teams.

Bullfighting *(corrida)* is also popular among Spaniards and tourists alike. However, it is as much an art as a sport to Spaniards. Foreign spectators often cannot understand the response of the crowd to what is happening in the arena.

Until a few years ago, most Spaniards would rather have watched sports than play them. Today, sports are not limited to the rich. Spaniards have begun to enjoy such sports as tennis, golf, fishing, skiing, and sailing. As in the past, Spaniards also enjoy many other forms of recreation. These include going to the movies, going for walks with friends, and talking in bars and cafes. These are all very sociable things to do, and Spaniards generally like being around people.

The Rastro flea market in Madrid, a favorite with residents and visitors alike.

Population and Ethnic Groups

The population of Spain is around 38 million. The people are mostly of mixed Mediterranean and northern European descent.

The Basques

Among the peoples of Spain are the Basques, the oldest surviving ethnic group in Europe. They speak a language of their own, and many call their homeland Euskalherria. Euskalherria is made up of the northern Basque provinces and parts of southern France.

There are many symbols of Basque life. One is the *frontón*, where the Basque game of *jai-alai* takes place. It represents sports. The church represents the deeply spiritual side of Basque life. It is Roman Catholic like all of Spain, but with spirits and witches from the regions's pagan past.

The center of the Basque family is the *basseria*, a three-story farmhouse. The structure of the Basque family is different from that of other Spanish families. Men and women are regarded as equal. Though they work at different jobs, they are considered of equal value. Family decisions take into account both men's and women's opinions.

The oak tree in the small town of Guernica is the symbolic heart of the Basque people. Under this tree, Spanish kings swore to defend Basque liberties in return for their support. During the Spanish Civil War, the Basques fought on the side of the government against the Fascist rebels. The town of Guernica was nearly destroyed by German Nazis in support of the rebels. The painting by artist Pablo Picasso, the *Guernica*, has shown millions of people all over the world the horrors of war. The

54

Guernica hung for many years in the Museum of Modern Art in New York. Today it is in the Prado, Spain's national art museum.

For thousands of years, Basque society remained stable. Property was passed on to the oldest son, so land stayed within families. In the middle ages, the French and Spanish kings granted the Basques independence. They had their own courts, currency, army, and parliament. In time, France and Spain each had a central government. France and Spain became single countries, and not groupings of separate states. Basque regional independence, or autonomy, was lost.

Spain's Basques have traditionally been among the wealthiest Spaniards. In 1900, almost all rich Spaniards were Basque. Today the region has lost much of its wealth as poor farmers from other regions come to look for work. Unemployment has become very high. Also, since the Civil War, the Spanish government has repressed Basque dissent. Repression and a desire for a united homeland have led to a movement to form a separate Basque state. This separatist movement has unified young Basques in the cities. Today Basque dances, sports, poetry, song, and language are becoming widespread once again.

The Basque separatist movement has also led to terror and violence. One organization, the ETA, has been responsible for more than five hundred murders since 1970. For many years, France has given shelter to Spanish Basques who were wanted in Spain. As the violence spreads to France, however, the French have become less tolerant of these people.

Since Franco's death, the Basque area has become more Socialist, like the rest of Spain. Basque political parties are becoming less unified. This has cut down their political power. The distance between the moderate Basques and the ETA has increased. The moderates are happier being part of Spain. The ETA has become more separatist than ever.

The Catalans

Besides the Basques, Spain's other minority group is the Catalans. They, too, have their own language. Both Spanish and Catalan are official languages of the Catalonian region. For seven short years during the Spanish Civil War, Catalonians proclaimed their independence as the Republic of Catalonia. Here they fought against the Fascist forces, but they lost. Many refugees fled to France. Those who remained were severely repressed by the Franco regime. The language was banned, and all Catalan street names were changed.

Today, Catalan is taught in the schools and is spoken by 17% of the Spanish population. The language is over 1000 years old and has changed very little. Once it was the language of law and government. It is today the language of everyday speech.

The Catalans also have a separatist movement. But more support is given to the movement to preserve the culture than to gain political independence. Catalonia was once a world power. The pride in their history has a strong hold on Catalans. Soccer games between the Barcelona football club and other Spanish teams are a time for displays of Catalan pride.

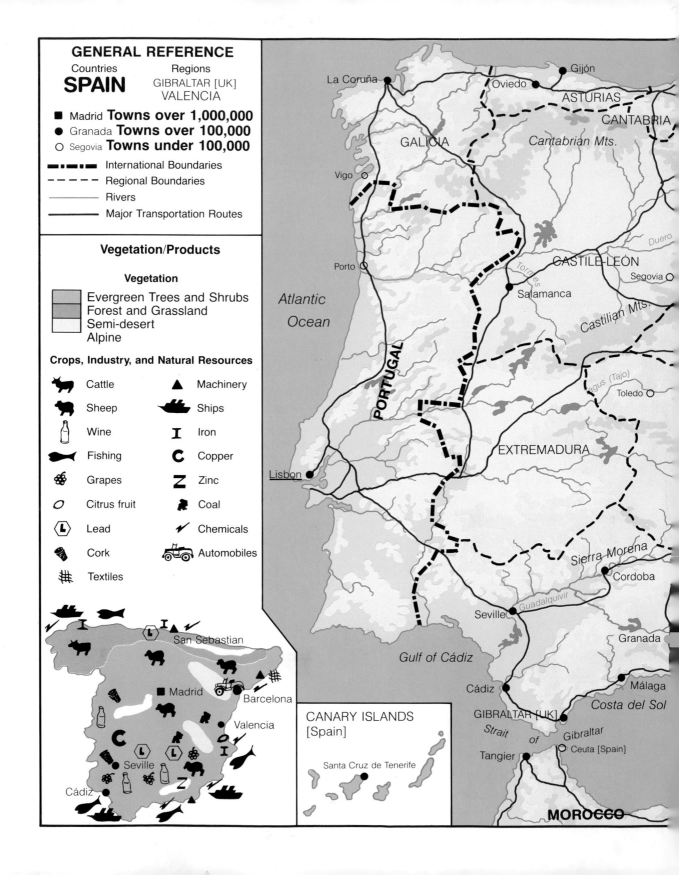

GENERAL REFERENCE

Countries
SPAIN

Regions
GIBRALTAR [UK]
VALENCIA

■ Madrid **Towns over 1,000,000**
● Granada **Towns over 100,000**
○ Segovia **Towns under 100,000**

▬▪▬▪▬ International Boundaries
▬ ▬ ▬ Regional Boundaries
──── Rivers
──── Major Transportation Routes

Vegetation/Products

Vegetation

Evergreen Trees and Shrubs
Forest and Grassland
Semi-desert
Alpine

Crops, Industry, and Natural Resources

Cattle   ▲ Machinery
Sheep   Ships
Wine   I Iron
Fishing   C Copper
Grapes   Z Zinc
Citrus fruit   Coal
Lead   Chemicals
Cork   Automobiles
Textiles

La Coruña
Gijón
Oviedo
ASTURIAS
CANTABRIA
GALICIA
Cantabrian Mts.
Vigo
Duero
CASTILE-LEÓN
Segovia
Porto
Tormes
Salamanca
Castilian Mts.
Atlantic Ocean
Tagus (Tajo)
Toledo
PORTUGAL
EXTREMADURA
Lisbon
Sierra Morena
Cordoba
Guadalquivir
Seville
Granada
Gulf of Cádiz
Cádiz
Málaga
Costa del Sol
GIBRALTAR [UK]
Strait of Gibraltar
Tangier
Ceuta [Spain]
MOROCCO

San Sebastian
■ Madrid
Barcelona
Valencia
Seville
Cádiz

CANARY ISLANDS
[Spain]

Santa Cruz de Tenerife

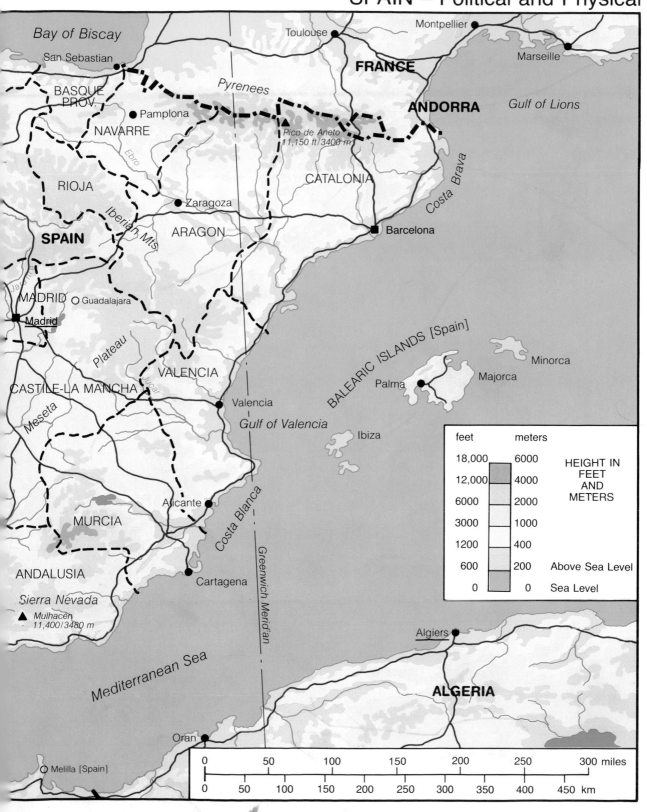

SPAIN – Political and Physical

Bay of Biscay

Montpellier

San Sebastian

FRANCE

Toulouse

Marseille

BASQUE PROV.

Pyrenees

ANDORRA

Gulf of Lions

Pamplona

NAVARRE

▲ *Pico de Aneto 11,150 ft / 3400 m*

RIOJA

CATALONIA

Ebro

Costa Brava

Iberian Mts.

Zaragoza

SPAIN

ARAGON

Barcelona

Jalon

MADRID

○ Guadalajara

BALEARIC ISLANDS [Spain]

■ Madrid

Minorca

Plateau

Palma

Majorca

Meseta

Jucar

VALENCIA

CASTILE-LA MANCHA

Valencia

Gulf of Valencia

Ibiza

feet   meters

MURCIA

Alicante

18,000   6000   HEIGHT IN FEET AND METERS

Costa Blanca

12,000   4000

ANDALUSIA

6000   2000

Sierra Nevada

3000   1000

Greenwich Meridian

▲ *Mulhacén 11,400 / 3480 m*

1200   400

600   200   Above Sea Level

Cartagena

0   0   Sea Level

Algiers

Mediterranean Sea

ALGERIA

0   50   100   150   200   250   300 miles

Oran

0   50   100   150   200   250   300   350   400   450 km

○ Melilla [Spain]

57

Land

Most of Spain shares the Iberian Peninsula with its neighbor to the west, Portugal. Its northeast border is with France. Sandwiched between France and Spain in the Pyrenees Mountains is tiny Andorra. At Spain's southern tip is Gibraltar. Gibraltar is a tiny British possession. The government often claims it should be part of Spain. Across the narrow Strait of Gibraltar is Morocco, in North Africa.

Spain includes the Balearic Islands in the Mediterranean Sea and the Canary Islands in the Atlantic Ocean off Africa. Including the Balearics and Canaries, Spain's total area is 195,988 sq miles (507,606 sq km). This is about the size of Utah and Arizona combined, or slightly smaller than the Yukon Territory.

Surrounded by water on three sides and the Pyrenees Mountains in the north, the Iberian Peninsula is cut off from the rest of Europe. Spain's interior has many mountains and high plateaus which rise sharply from the sea. The Meseta Plateau, in the center of Spain, covers more than 50% of the country's area. It is the largest plateau of its kind in Europe. And next to Switzerland, Spain has the second highest average elevation in Europe, 2200 ft (670 m). Spain's mountains, plateaus, and rivers form natural barriers for the many regions and peoples within Spain.

Climate

Almost three-quarters of Spain is quite dry, with less than 20 inches (50 cm) of rain per year. The coastal areas in the east and south are like most places along the Mediterranean: hot and dry for a long time in the summer and somewhat milder in the winter. Temperatures in northwest Spain vary more than in other areas, and there is rain year round. In the center of the country, around Madrid in the Meseta Plateau, the climate is dry, with hot summers and cold winters.

Industry, Agriculture, and Natural Resources

Since 1979, dry weather and rising costs have cut down on Spain's farm production. Agriculture is still an important part of Spain's economy, however. Along with such minerals as iron, copper, zinc, and lead, agricultural products make up much of Spain's exports. When crops are good, Spain can provide food for itself with few imports from other countries. Important agricultural products include cattle, sheep, wine grapes, and fish. Spain is the sixth largest maker of wine in the world and the tenth largest catcher of fish. Spain's crops include fruits, vegetables, and grains.

Spain's leading industries include automobiles, steel and iron, and clothing and other textiles. The automobile industry is expanding quickly. This is mainly because Ford and General Motors have built plants in Spain. Spain also produces machinery, ships, and chemicals. Most of Spain's industry has been around the northeast and the Atlantic coast. But the government has brought some industry into southern Spain and other less developed areas. Tourism has also been a major industry in Spain. In 1948, only about 148,000 tourists visited Spain annually. Today, more tourists visit Spain than any other country in the world — 45 million each year!

Spain's main trading partners are other Western European countries. The US is also a major trading partner at about 10% of Spain's import and export trading. Since the death of dictator Francisco Franco, Spain has tried to improve its economic standing in the world. One way of doing this has been to sell more to and buy less from industrialized nations such as the US and Canada. Spain has also tried to develop more technological industries. It has made great gains in high technology. But one price it has had to pay for greater technology in industry has been higher unemployment. Its unemployment rate in 1986 was 25%.

The Plaza Mayor, once the scene of bullfights, tournaments, and, during the Spanish Inquisition, religious trials. In modern days, it bustled with cars, trolleys, and buses until the 1970s. Today, it is open only to pedestrians and is one of Madrid's most beautiful and famous squares.

Madrid

With a population of 3.5 million, Madrid is the largest city in Spain. Located in the center of the Iberian Peninsula, it became the capital in 1561. Today it is surrounded by an industrial belt 20 miles (32km) deep. Closer to the center of the city, high-rise housing and industrial buildings give way to other sights. Madrid has tree-lined boulevards, large fountains, parks, circles, plazas, and modern hotels and shops. Its sidewalk cafes and flea markets attract visitors and residents of Madrid.

Another favorite attraction is the Casa de la Villa, Madrid's City Hall. It is a small Renaissance palace. The Palacio Real - Royal Palace - was finished in 1764. It provided a home for Spanish monarchs for almost two hundred years. Tours through the Royal Palace show 50 of its nearly 2000 rooms. Today, King Juan Carlos and Queen Sophia live in the Palacio de la Zarzuela, just outside Madrid. The top spot on any tourist's trip to Madrid would be the Museo del Prado, Madrid's world-famous art museum. The Prado's collection consists of 3000 works of art.

Spanish People in North America

Spaniards have settled all over the world, and today Spanish is spoken by 300 million people in 21 countries. Spanish emigration started with the discovery of the Americas, including parts of what are now the southern, southwestern, and western US. During the American Revolution, Spaniards in the New World lent military and financial help to the Anglo American colonies in their fight against Britain.

The language, customs, and religion of Latinos - North Americans of Hispanic descent - began with the Spanish conquerors and settlers. Today, Latino culture is a special blend of *many* American cultures, including Afro-American, American Indian, Anglo, Cuban, Mexican, Puerto Rican, and South and Central American. About 60% of all Hispanic Americans in North America are of Mexican descent; about 30% are Puerto Rican; 3-5% are Cuban. The remaining 5-7% are mainly Central American.

There are also other communities in North America that are Spanish in origin. They trace their roots to the original Spaniards from Europe, not to a mixture of Spanish, Indian, and Mexican. They refer to themselves as *Spanish* rather than Hispanic or Latino. They live mainly in California, where they also call themselves *Californios*, and in New Mexico and Arizona.

Today, some Spaniards leave Spain to earn a better living. Of those that leave, around 62% come to the Americas. Most come to such Latin American countries as Argentina, Venezuela, and Uruguay. Many also come to North America, however. In the US, there are 140,000 Spanish immigrants. In Canada, there are 25,000.

Currency

The monetary unit in Spain is the *peseta*. It comes in coins of 1, 2½, 5, 25, 50, and 100 pesetas, and in bills of 100, 500, 1000, and 5000 pesetas.

Glossary of Useful Spanish Terms

Spain is a country of many regions and peoples, and of many dialects and languages. The official Spanish dialect is Castilian. This is the dialect that is used in the pronunciation guide that follows. You may notice that Castilian Spanish is different from the kind of Spanish you use or hear in the Americas.

adios (ah-DYOS) . . . . good-bye
aficionado (ah-FEE-thee-oh-NAH-doh) . . . . a devoted follower or fan
beisbol (BAZE-bol) . . . . baseball
bocadillo (bo-cah-DEE-oh) . . . . a crusty Spanish bread
carne (CAR-neh) . . . . meat
casa (CAH-sah) . . . . house
churro (CHURR-oh) . . . . a fried pastry
cocido (coh-THEE-doh) . . . . a meat and bean stew
corrida (coh-RREE-dah) . . . . "running"; bullfighting
Don (don) . . . . title of respect for men
used before first name only
Doña (DOH-nyah) . . . . title of respect for women
used before first name only
fiesta (fee-ES-tah) . . . . a holiday or festival
frito (FREE-toh) . . . . fried
frontón (fron-TON) . . . . jai-alai court
fútbol (FOOT-bol) . . . . football, or soccer
galleta (gah-YEH-ta) . . . . cookie
jai-alai (HI-ah-li) . . . . a Basque game played against a
tall wall with a ball and hand-
held basket

merienda (mare-ee-EN-dah). . . . . afternoon snack
paella (pah-AY-ah). . . . . a rice dish with meat
patata (peh-TAH-teh). potato
pelota (pay-LOH-tah). . . . . the Basque game of jai-alai
pipas (PEEP-ahs). . . . . sunflower seeds
plaza (PLAH-tha). . . . . public place or square
sefardi (seh-FAR-dee). . . . . Sephardic, or Spanish Jewish
siesta (see-ES-tah). . . . . afternoon nap or rest
tortilla (tor-TEE-yah) . . . . Spanish pancake

More Books About Spain

Here are some more books about Spain. If you are interested in them, check your library. They may be helpful in doing research for the following "Things to Do" projects.

The Land and People of Spain. Loder (Lippincott)
Let's Travel to Spain. Geis (Childrens Press)
Life in Europe: Spain. Maiques (Fideler)
Looking at Spain. Martin (Lippincott)
Take a Trip to Spain. Rutland (Watts)
My Village in Spain. Gidal (Pantheon)

Things to Do - Research Projects

Political, economic, and social conditions in Spain have changed dramatically since the death of dictator Francisco Franco in 1975. As you read about Spain, or any country, keep in mind the importance of current facts. Some of the research projects that follow need accurate, up-to-date information from current sources. Two publications your library may have will tell you about recent newspaper and magazine articles on many topics:

Readers' Guide to Periodical Literature

Children's Magazine Guide

For accurate answers to questions about such topics of current interest as Spain's efforts to make progress as a member of the European community, look up *Spain* in these two publications. They will lead you to the most up-to-date information you can find.

1. In some countries, portions of the population wish to secede, or withdraw, from the government that rules them. They may wish to secede for political, religious, or cultural reasons. Some better known examples include French Canadians in Québec, Sikhs in India, and Catholics in Northern Ireland who want to join the Irish Republic to the south. Using current sources in the library, compare one of these movements to the Basque movement in Spain.

2. Use your library resources to learn about Islam and Judaism in Spain. What are the lasting influences of these two cultures in Catholic Spain today?

3. Think of an occupation or career that interests you. Would you be able to do this in Spain? Would being male or female make a difference? Use recent sources of information from the library.

4. Imagine that you are taking a bus trip through Spain. Plan the route you would take. Write an imaginary diary about what you see. Include descriptions of the land, rivers, climate, historical landmarks, and people.

More Things to Do - Activities

These projects are designed to encourage you to think more about Spain. They offer ideas for interesting group or individual projects for school or home.

1. Why do you think it is important to study the history of Spain to understand it today?

2. Write an imaginary letter to Felisa. Explain how your life compares with hers and ask her any questions you'd like about her life in Andalusia.

3. Spain's empire once covered much of the Americas. In what ways that you can think of has Spain made a difference in your country?

4. If you would like a pen pal in Spain, write to these people:

International Pen Friends
P.O. Box 290065
Brooklyn, NY 11229-0001

Be sure to tell them what country you want your pen pal to be from. Also include your full name and address.

Index